Ready to Go

Devotions

For Mission & Service

Contents

Ready to Go

Introduction

"Go therefore and make disciples of all nations, baptizing them in the name of the Father and of the Son and of the Holy Spirit."

—*Matthew 28:19*

As Christians, we're called to go and make disciples. As youth workers, we often answer that call through mission trips and work projects. We load our students into minivans, tour buses, and airplanes. We haul them to nearby cities, distant states, and countries halfway around the globe. We spend a day feeding the homeless, a weekend repairing houses, or a week running a Bible school. We apply bandages, soothe tempers, and treat homesickness with hugs.

And then we come home.

What have we accomplished? Perhaps we've helped a homeless man survive another day. Perhaps we've given an older adult a roof that doesn't leak. Perhaps we've taken the gospel to a child who has never heard about Jesus.

That's all great stuff (Great Commission stuff, in fact). But what about our students? Has the experience changed them? Have they received as much love as they've given? Have they become the disciples you set out to make?

HIGH HORSES AND HIGH ROLLERS

While on youth mission trips over the years, I've noticed a couple of phenomena. Some students (and many adults) have a knights-in-shining-armor attitude of pride and self-righteousness. They swoop into the mission field on their noble steeds, do some good work, and gallop off into the sunset. Their armor shields them from the people they're serving and keeps the Holy Spirit from entering their hearts.

And then there's the Vegas attitude—you know, what happens in Vegas stays in Vegas. Many students are happy to go without showers for a couple of days, love on little kids, and even shed a few tears; but once they get back home, back to "reality," they revert to their pre-trip, business-as-usual selves.

We're as much to blame as the students are for this attitude. If we don't get our students off their high horses, we've missed a chance to help them let God transform their lives. If they don't bring home more than just dirty laundry, we've failed to fully live out the Great Commission.

CAPTURING THE MOMENTS

We can't script life-changing moments, of course. We can't decide that on Tuesday at 1:17 P.M.—right between lunch and our afternoon work project—our students will finally "get it." The Holy Spirit just doesn't stick to human schedules.

But we don't need to create those moments; we just need to capture them when they happen. We need to build into our mission trips and service projects opportunities for students (and chaperones) to reflect on what they're experiencing.

That's the point of this book. In the following pages, you'll find dozens of daily devotions that relate to specific issues: spiritual baggage, language barriers, host families, schedule changes, homesickness, differences in culture, lack of sleep, and so on. Each devotion ties together three elements: Scripture, the mission or service experience, and life back home. Students are challenged not just to read the devotions but also to respond to them through writing, reflection, and prayer. By working through the devotions, students should be able to think about their experiences and start their days better equipped for service. They should also learn some important lessons they can take home along with their snapshots, sunburns, and smelly laundry.

> **Each devotion ties together three elements:**
>
> • **Scripture,**
>
> • **the mission or service experience, and**
>
> • **life back home.**

Most mission trips and work projects are whirlwinds of activity. But as **1 Kings 19:11-12** reminds us, God is not always in the whirlwind. Sometimes we need to slow down and listen for God's still, small voice. My prayer is that these devotions help you and your students do just that.

Now, go and make disciples!

WHAT THIS BOOK CONTAINS

As you've probably figured out by now, this book and the accompanying CD-ROM include devotions for both multi-day mission trips and one-day service projects. Each devotion has its own unique theme (identified in the Table of Contents), and each is completely independent of the others. Since the devotions don't build on or refer to one another, you can use them in any order and assortment.

For mission trips, you'll find five pre-trip devotions, twenty-seven on-trip devotions, and five post-trip devotions.

For service projects, you'll find five pre-service devotions and five post-service devotions. There are no "during" devotions, since one-day projects rarely allow much time for reflection; however, you could easily use a post-service devotion at the end of a work day if time allows.

Each devotion include four sections:

➜ **Read** (a Scripture passage related to the theme);

➜ **Reflect** (a commentary on the passage and how it relates to the mission or service experience);

➜ **React** (a theme-specific life application, along with space for taking notes);

➜ **Prayer Focus** (a topic to pray about that day, again related to the theme).

The CD-ROM gives you all of the devotions in this book in a digital format, along with resources to help you create custom devotional books for your youth and their parents. It also includes a road-bingo game and a "cootie catcher" that youth can fold and use as a discussion starter.

HOW TO USE THIS BOOK

The devotions in this book are designed for individual use, but you could easily adapt them for group use. The devotions are also flexible enough to be used in the morning or the evening, depending on your schedule. Below are some specific ideas for using them.

BEFORE AND AFTER YOUR TRIP OR PROJECT

The purpose of the pre-trip and pre-service devotions is to ease your students into the mission or work experience. The post-trip and post-service devotions give you a few last chances to connect the experience with life at home. Before and after each trip or project, you'll have five devotions to choose from, but you'll probably need fewer.

Here are some ideas for pre-trip and pre-service devotions:

→ Send out a devotion via mail or e-mail two weeks and one week before your trip or work project.

→ Include a devotion in mailings about your mission trip or service project.

→ If you hold a covenant or commissioning meeting prior to your trip or project, read and discuss a devotion during that meeting.

→ Have mission moments at youth group meetings prior to your trip or project. This method can help you reach students who aren't going to be participating.

For the post-trip and post-service devotions:

→ Send out a devotion via mail or e-mail one week and two weeks after your trip or work project. Include a photo or two from that experience.

→ If you have a follow-up meeting or celebration after your trip or project, read and discuss a devotion during that meeting.

→ Have mission moments at youth group meetings after your trip or project. Again, this method can help you reach students who didn't participate (and possibly get them excited about future mission opportunities).

DURING YOUR MISSION TRIP

The on-trip devotions are the heart of this book. Using them can be more meaningful—and more complicated—than using the before and after materials.

Devotional Booklets for the Youth

Select the devotion that seems right for each day.

The best way to use the on-trip devotions is to create a booklet that includes one devotion for each day of the trip. Don't just pick a random assortment of devotions, however. Instead, think and pray about the trip you've planned; then select the devotion that seems right for each day.

For Day 1, you might pick a devotion about setting out on a journey; for Day 2, one about dealing with people who are different. If you're going overseas, you might choose "Say What?" (page 30), which deals with language barriers. If you know that the housing accommodations on Day 5 will be pretty rugged, consider using "No Place to Lay His Head" (page 68) that day. Spend some time on these decisions, and you'll be pleasantly surprised at how clearly you hear God's voice.

With a little extra work, your booklet of devotions can become a full-fledged trip journal. In the front, stick your trip covenant, schedule, emergency contact information, housing assignments, fun facts about the places you're visiting, and so forth. In the back, add some blank pages for journaling. Slap on cardstock covers, run the whole thing through a comb binder, and you'll have a product that your students will not only use but keep. (The CD-ROM has some sample pages to get you started.)

If you'd rather use the devotions in a group setting, take this book along with you on the trip. Pick a devotion for each evening's group meeting that matches the events of the day. Have one student read the Scripture, another the commentary, and a third the React section. Discuss the questions as a group, keeping in mind that some responses may be too personal to reveal.

A few more points:

→ The devotions are designed to be as general as possible. If you have the time, customize them by sticking in references to the places you're going and the specific work you're doing.

→ The devotions don't work without Bibles! If you aren't taking Bibles along (due to space constraints or whatever), add the relevant Scriptures to the devotions in your booklets.

The devotions won't work without Bibles!

→ For best results, build consistent devotional time into your schedule, whether it's the ten minutes after breakfast each day or the half-hour before bedtime. Don't just assume that the students will do their daily devotions on their own.

→ If you create devotional booklets, make enough copies for your students' parents. Many of them will appreciate the chance to do the devotions back home while you're doing them on the trip. This method can also give the students and parents a basis for meaningful discussions after the trip—and will show the parents how on the ball you are!

In the end, what matters is not which method you choose to do the devotions. What matters is how you invite God to use them to work in the lives of your students, your chaperones, and you.

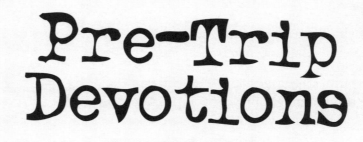

Pre-Trip Devotions

TRAVELING LIGHTLY

FOCUS: Beginnings

READ: Mark 6:6b-13

REFLECT

Jesus wanted his disciples to be more than mere followers; he wanted them to be his representatives in the world. So he sent them out in pairs to preach the gospel, perform miracles, and heal the sick.

Jesus told the disciples to travel lightly—no food, no money, just the clothes on their backs. He wanted them to rely on the hospitality of the people they encountered along the way, and he knew they'd make more progress if they weren't burdened with a lot of baggage.

And progress they made. Even though they didn't have their stuff, they did just what Jesus called them to do.

REACT

Traveling lightly is still a good idea today. Hardcore backpackers, for instance, sometimes saw off the handles of their toothbrushes and leave their flashlights and spare underwear at home. They don't want to deal with all that extra weight.

Though weight usually isn't an issue on mission trips, we all tend to carry around spiritual baggage: broken relationships, anger, addictive behaviors, selfishness, misplaced priorities, and cliques. And they slow us down just as much as a boat anchor would slow down a backpacker.

Like Jesus' disciples, we've been commissioned to spend the days ahead sharing the gospel with people who desperately need Christ in their lives.

What spiritual baggage are you tempted to bring on the trip that might prevent you from doing what God is calling you to do? What do you need to leave at home (or maybe abandon at our first rest stop)? How can you do so?

Notes

HERE I AM

FOCUS: Your unique mission

READ: Isaiah 6:1-8; 1 Corinthians 12:12-26

REFLECT

The passage from Isaiah tells a strange story. Isaiah, this "man of unclean lips," saw the Lord in all God's glory seated on God's throne. The air was full of smoke, angels, and (we can imagine) the sound of trumpets blaring a heavenly fanfare. Why did God appear to Isaiah? Because God was looking for a volunteer to do a tough job—to go and tell Israel some hard truths. The prophet immediately raised his hand and said, "Here I am."

Isaiah wasn't the only individual whom God equipped for a unique mission. As Paul tells us, each person in the church is called to serve. In his first letter to the Corinthians, Paul built an analogy between the church and the human body. Both are units made up of lots of different parts, each of which has a unique and essential purpose. A body made entirely of ears cannot function; and an ear cannot decide that it would rather be an eye and leave its body. Later in the chapter, Paul talks about some of the many gifts that members of the church have: leadership, teaching, healing, and so on. Again, each of these gifts is essential to the church's success.

REACT

In a group like ours, thinking that your individual contribution doesn't matter can be easy. If you don't have the right skills or you don't know the Bible backwards and forwards or if you're—gasp!—a sinner, then how important can you be?

Incredibly important. God may place someone in your path during our trip whom you, and only you, can minister to. The person may be someone at a worksite, someone you encounter on the street, or even another group member. Whoever it is, you may be uniquely qualified to reach out to him or her.

Take a few minutes to reflect on the unique qualities you possess. What about you—your age, your heritage, your interests, or maybe your weaknesses—can God use to reach others?

Notes

HOW CAN I UNDERSTAND?

FOCUS: Being ready to witness

READ: Acts 8:26-39

REFLECT

In the Acts of the Apostles, Jesus' disciples traveled the countryside, spreading the gospel (literally the "good news") about Jesus. Many of them had encountered the risen Christ, and they were eager to share their faith in him with anyone ready to listen.

One person who was ready was the Ethiopian government official found in **Acts 8.** As his chariot rolled away from Jerusalem, he read from **Isaiah 53,** which prophesied that the long hoped-for Messiah would be "led like a sheep to the slaughter." When Philip popped up and asked whether the Ethiopian understood the reading, the official replied, "How can I unless someone explains it to me?"

Fortunately, Philip was ready. He used the Ethiopian's question and the passage from Isaiah as an opening to share the gospel and talk about his faith in Jesus. In the end, the Ethiopian asked Philip to baptize him and then went on his way, rejoicing.

REACT

On this trip, you may meet a person who needs you to be his or her Philip. It might be a lifelong Christian who's curious about why you look so joyful. It may be someone who's never set foot in a church and wants to know why you're spending time working in her community. It may be a fellow group member who's ready to go deeper in his faith.

When someone asks you to talk about Jesus, you're going to have an opportunity to change that person's life—if you're ready. You don't have to have all the answers or be able to spout a bunch of theological statements; but you do need to be prepared to honestly and openly share your faith. Make some notes on the next page about what you might say.

There's one more lesson in the story of Philip and the Ethiopian. Go back to Acts, and notice who spoke first. Yep, it was Philip. The Ethiopian's question came only after Philip asked, "Do you understand what you are reading?"

Part of your job as a Philip is not just to answer questions but also to ask a few of your own. Not sure what to ask? Start with names or sports or the weather. With the simplest questions, you can open doors and create relationships that could eventually send people on their way rejoicing.

Prayer Focus

Pray for the strength to ask some questions and the wisdom to answer others.

Notes

ALL THINGS TO ALL PEOPLE

FOCUS: Finding common ground

READ: 1 Corinthians 9:19-23

REFLECT

Paul was uniquely qualified to spread the gospel to the Gentiles (non-Jews). Unlike Peter and the other original disciples, Paul was a well-traveled, well-educated Roman citizen. As a Jew, he understood the roots of Christianity. As a Roman, he understood how to spread the Christian gospel throughout the empire.

One of his techniques, as he explained his first letter to the church at Corinth, was to use every part of himself for the sake of the gospel. To the Jews, he was like a Jew. To the Gentiles, he was like someone not bound by Jewish law. To the weak, he exposed his weaknesses.

Paul didn't pretend to be something he wasn't. Instead, he revealed everything he was. In doing so, he found things he had in common with people who were different from him; and he allowed the Holy Spirit to use those commonalities to bring people to Christ.

REACT

If you don't find people who are vastly different from you on this trip, it'll be because you aren't paying attention. The people you're going to serve are very different. So are your chaperones and even your friends.

The first step in reaching out to people who are different from you is to find things you have in common. Like Paul, you are the sum of all your experiences, a unique combination of strengths and weaknesses, skills and shortcomings, hopes and fears. And there's something about you—something in you—that God can use to connect with someone during this trip. All you have to do is find it and reveal it.

Think about the people you're going to serve: their culture, religion, language, economic status, politics, hobbies, and so on. Now think about yourself. On the next page, write down some areas where you think your life might intersect with theirs.

Notes

WHAT'S YOUR STORY?

FOCUS: Writing your testimony

READ: 1 Corinthians 15:1-11

REFLECT

Besides being a tireless apostle, Paul was an advice columnist of all sorts. His letters to the church at Corinth, written a few years after his visit to that city, are full of detailed advice about specific problems the church was having.

But this passage doesn't deal with specific problems. Instead, it focuses on the core truth of the Christian faith: that Christ died for our sins and was resurrected on the third day.

Most likely, **1 Corinthians 15:3-7** is an early Christian creed, or statement of faith, that stresses the importance of receiving and transmitting holy truths.

In verse 8, Paul included himself in the creed's list of people who had a personal encounter with the resurrected Christ. In doing so, he emphasized that he hadn't just heard about the Resurrection but had experienced it.

REACT

During our mission trip, you may have the chance to share Christ with people who've never encountered him before. Your chance may come in a formal setting, such as a worship service, or more informally around the dinner table. Whenever it comes, you need to be ready.

Take some time now to write on the next page your own testimony about experiencing Christ. Start with familiar Scriptures (such as **John 3:16**) or standards of faith (such as the Apostle's Creed), but don't stop there. Note some of the ways Christ has touched your life, the way you've been changed by your relationship with him. Practice and polish your testimony so that you're ready to give it at a moment's notice.

Prayer Focus

Pray that God will use you to spread the good news to people who need to hear it.

Notes

Ready to Go

On-Trip Devotions

GETTING DOWN OUT OF THE BOAT

FOCUS: Trust in Christ

READ: Matthew 14:22-33

REFLECT

The story of Peter trying—and failing—to walk on water is a familiar one. The disciples had been out in a boat waiting for Jesus, who came walking across the lake toward them. They were all terrified, thinking they'd seen a ghost. But then Peter got out of the boat, walked toward Jesus, and started to sink. "Lord, save me!" he cried out—perhaps the Bible's shortest and simplest prayer.

Most of us would react to Peter the same way Jesus did, accusing Peter of having too little faith in his Master. But think about this question: Who else got out of the boat? Who else was willing to walk toward Jesus, harnessing, for however short a time, a little of his awesome power?

REACT

We all have times in our lives when we need to get down out of the boat. Perhaps you're nervous about the projects you'll be working on today. Perhaps this trip is bringing up relational or personal issues that you need to finally start dealing with. Perhaps these matters are waiting for you back home. You know you need to take that first step, but you just don't know where to find the strength.

As Peter discovered, that strength lies in Christ. Keep your eyes focused on him, and you'll be fine. And if you happen to look at the wind and the waves instead, he'll be close by to catch you.

Sometimes, we need to name our demons to tame our demons. Write down the areas in your life where you need Christ to support you today.

Prayer Focus

In what way do you need to get down out of the boat? Pray about that situation, asking for the strength and support that can come only from Christ. Picture him holding out a hand ready to catch you and keep you from falling . . . and failing.

Notes

MUTUALLY ENCOURAGED

FOCUS: Being served by those we serve

READ: Romans 1:8-12

REFLECT

By the time Paul wrote his letter to the Romans, he'd been a Christian for twenty years. His first three missionary journeys were behind him, and he had plenty to be proud of. But he hadn't made it to Rome yet. Like an actor who hasn't reached Hollywood or a politician who hasn't gotten to Washington, D.C., Paul longed to visit Rome, the seat of power, the hub of the empire.

He would get there a few years later, but Christianity beat him to the capital. In fact, the Roman Christians' faith was being reported "all over the world," although plenty of work was yet to be done there. Paul looked forward not just to strengthening the Roman Christians but to being strengthened by them. He longed to see them so that he and they might "be mutually encouraged by each other's faith" (**Romans 1:12**).

REACT

When we go on mission trips, we often imagine ourselves taking Christ to people for the first time. But the truth is that Christ is already there; the seeds of faith have already been planted. All we need to do is water them and nurture them and maybe pull a few weeds here and there.

And we ourselves have the chance to be watered and nurtured, to have the weeds pulled out from around our faith. We're here to serve, but don't be surprised if someone serves *you.* In that way, we can all be mutually encouraged by one another's faith.

Take a few minutes to write (on the next page) ways you need to be encouraged in your faith today. Do you ever find yourself putting up barriers to the help that other people offer? What are those barriers? How could you lower them and let the help flow in?

Notes

BACK IN EGYPT

FOCUS: Remembering our blessings

READ: Exodus 16:1-5

REFLECT

By the sixteenth chapter of Exodus, the journey out of Egypt had finally begun. After centuries of bondage, Pharaoh had finally let God's people go, and they had started walking toward the Promised Land.

This passage picks up the story one month into the trip, when the Israelites weren't very happy. The Scripture says the "whole community" was grumbling against their leaders, Moses and Aaron; some people were even openly saying they wished they were back in Egypt.

Back in Egypt?! Yep. After a few weeks of relatively minor suffering, they were ready to go back to Egypt, where they could again build cities for Pharaoh, get beaten by their overseers, make brick without straw, and watch their male newborns being thrown into the Nile. But even in the midst of their ingratitude, God provided them, literally, with their daily bread.

REACT

We all act like those grumbling Israelites from time to time. We get so accustomed to the many blessings in our lives that we focus on what we don't have instead of thanking God for what we do have. We're like the man who complained he had no shoes until he saw a man who had no feet.

Ingratitude can creep up on us during mission trips. Long hours on the road, too little sleep, and too much togetherness can all magnify the problems we face. But the people we're here to serve and work with—people who have plenty of legitimate things to grumble about but are generally more grateful for what they do have—should prompt us to focus on our blessings instead.

Take a moment to list the blessings you're enjoying on this trip and those that await you back home.

Prayer Focus

Do you feel like a grumbling Israelite today? Do you find yourself doubting that God will supply your every need? Take a few moments to thank God for the blessings in your life.

Notes

SOLD INTO SLAVERY

FOCUS: Finding God in suffering

READ: Genesis 37:17b-28; 45:4-10

REFLECT

If there was ever someone who didn't want to go on a journey, it was Joseph. Back in **Genesis 37,** this son of Jacob was happy flitting around in his "amazing Technicolor dreamcoat"(as a famous musical describes it) and having prophetic dreams about his eleven brothers all bowing down to him like many sheaves of grain. But then his brothers sold him into slavery, as the first passage recounts. He eventually ended up in Egypt, where he and his dreams seemed likely to die in jail.

But God wasn't done with Joseph. Through a series of "happy accidents" (which weren't really accidents but acts of God), the dreamer came to the attention of Pharaoh, a man whose dreams weren't quite as pleasant as the ones Joseph had enjoyed. Joseph interpreted Pharaoh's dreams as a prediction of a seven-year famine, told him how to prepare, and promptly got promoted to the post of Pharaoh's second-in-command.

Suffering from the famine, Joseph's brothers had come to Egypt to buy food, as **Genesis 45** shows. After reuniting with Joseph (whom they'd figured was dead), he helped them, forgave them for their past misdeeds, and showed them how God had been at work throughout the story.

REACT

God doesn't cause suffering, but God can certainly use it for good. For the ultimate example, just look at the cross.

You may be suffering right now, either from temporary problems on this trip or more persistent problems you'll have to face when you get home. How can God help you through your suffering and make good things come out of it? The song "Hymn of Promise" says "there's a dawn in every darkness." Where do you see a dawn in your darkness? Make some notes on the next page.

Prayer Focus

Pray that God might reveal God's plan for transforming your suffering into triumph the way the Lord did with Joseph.

Notes

SAY WHAT?

FOCUS: Language barriers

READ: Luke 10:25-37

REFLECT

Most of us are quite familiar with the parable of the good Samaritan. But we sometimes forget that Jesus originally told the story in response to a question: "Who is my neighbor?"

In fact, over and over again in the Gospels, Jesus answered a question by telling a story or by asking a question of his own. He did both of those things in this passage from Luke. He even wrapped up the parable with one last question: "Which of these three do you think was a neighbor to the man who fell into the hands of robbers?"

The answer to that question is obvious, but sometimes the answers aren't so clear. More than once, the disciples (Jesus' closest followers) came up after the crowds had left, and said, "Huh? We didn't quite get that one, boss. Can you run that past us again?"

As you can see, the disciples got pretty frustrated with Jesus sometimes. Why couldn't he just come right out and say what he meant? Why couldn't he speak their language?

Perhaps it was because he wanted them to think. If they had to come up with an answer on their own or decode a parable by themselves, they would better remember the truth he was trying to share.

REACT

One of the challenges of international mission trips is to overcome language barriers. Even if we've studied a foreign language in school for years, being immersed in a culture that speaks the language can be overwhelming. And so we get frustrated, wishing that everyone would just speak our language.

But words are just one way to communicate. Smiles, hugs, and handshakes work too. And if we have to try harder than usual to communicate, then maybe we learn an important truth: Our neighbors aren't just those people who speak our language. (That truth applies just as much back home as it does when traveling abroad.)

Write down some of the linguistic challenges you've faced so far on this trip. How have you overcome those challenges? What else could you do?

Prayer Focus

Pray that God might give you new ways to communicate with people who don't speak your language.

Notes

KEEP THE HOME FIRES BURNING

FOCUS: Those at home

READ: Acts 13:1-3; 14:26-28

REFLECT

Acts 13–14 tells of Paul's first great missionary journey, which lasted from roughly 46–48 B.C. and covered more than a thousand miles throughout the northeastern Mediterranean region. Our Scriptures for today are Luke's account of the beginning and end of that journey.

As **Acts 13** opens, we learn that Paul and Barnabas were among the key members of the church at Antioch (one of the earliest Christian communities), along with men named Simeon, Lucius, and Manaen. Through worship and prayer, the church recognized a need to send out missionaries; so it selected Paul and Barnabas. That decision made, the church fasted and prayed some more, blessed the missionaries, and sent them off.

Paul never forgot where he came from. During his trips, he remembered that he was representing his fellow Christians back home and that they were supporting him with their prayers. After each trip, he returned to Antioch to report what he'd accomplished. The Christians back home must have been thrilled to hear about his work. Undoubtedly, their faith was strengthened as they heard about Paul's accomplishments in far-flung places such as Perga, Lystra, and Iconium.

REACT

Like Paul, we're away from home but still know where our home is. We're strangers in a strange place (although not as strange as Perga, Lystra, or Iconium), but we know we're not alone. We have the support of parents, church leaders, and group members who couldn't make the trip. We're also backed by people whose financial giving made this trip possible. We have a responsibility to all of those people to represent them and our church well.

But we also have an opportunity to tell these people about our experiences. After the trip, we'll report back to our church in a formal presentation to our families and in casual conversations around the dinner table. Those encounters may be more subdued than the ones we have in the next few days on this mission trip, but they have just as much power to change a life forever. Who knows? You may convince a friend or family member to participate in a mission trip in the future.

Write down some stories you want to tell when you get home. Include as many details as possible so that you don't forget what happened. Add to this list throughout the trip.

Prayer Focus

Pray for those group members who couldn't make the trip and for the people who made sacrifices to enable us to do God's work through mission.

Notes

HOLY INTERRUPTIONS

FOCUS: Dealing with change

READ: Acts 9:1-19

REFLECT

After the stoning of Stephen, Christianity's first martyr, believers in Christ scattered throughout Judea and Samaria. Some had even gone as far as Damascus to escape persecution. But Saul, who would later become Paul, was hot on their trail. This self-appointed, one-man vigilante squad headed for Damascus, arrest warrants in hand, ready to chase down every last Christian—man, woman, or child.

Along the road to Damascus, Saul had a strange encounter. The risen Christ appeared to him and demanded, "Saul, Saul, why do you persecute me?" (**Acts 9:4b**). Saul was instantly blinded; but at the same time, the "eyes of [his] heart" opened (**Ephesians 1:18**). This persecutor of Christians had become the faith's greatest apostle, and history turned in a new direction.

REACT

A wise person (or perhaps just a wise guy) once said that the only person who likes change is a wet baby. But experienced missionaries know that change is inevitable. They even have a saying: "Blessed are the flexible, for they shall not be bent out of shape."

Saul certainly learned about change. Although he reached his planned destination, Damascus, that goal was probably the only thing that went according to plan.

Our plans for this trip will undoubtedly change, although probably not as drastically as Saul's did. Some of the changes may be mere inconveniences, but others will be holy interruptions. If we allow ourselves to live in those moments rather than rushing past them, we may, like Saul, reach our destination as changed people. And history may turn in a new direction.

How do you normally react to change? How have you dealt with unexpected events on this trip? If you don't handle change very well, what could you do to make yourself more open to holy interruptions both on this trip and back home? Make some notes on the next page.

Notes

THEY WERE ALL ENCOURAGED

FOCUS: Finding sabbath time

READ: Acts 27:27-36

REFLECT

Near the end of Acts, Paul had been arrested in Jerusalem for spreading the gospel. He had demanded a hearing before Caesar—something all Roman citizens have the right to do—and was on a ship bound for Rome.

The trip across the sea didn't go very smoothly. Paul's ship was caught in a nor'easter, and just about everyone gave up hope of being saved. The crew struggled to save the ship and even conspired to sneak away in a lifeboat.

Early one morning, after several days of raging storms, Paul urged everyone to take a break and have something to eat. The food and fellowship calmed and encouraged the group. That same day, they ran aground at Malta; and everyone reached land safely.

Prayer Focus

Pray for the sabbath time you need to recharge your spiritual batteries.

REACT

Just as making time to eat was difficult for the distressed sailors in Acts, finding time for food and fellowship can be difficult when we're on a mission trip. Finding time to rest and pray can also be a challenge. Amid our busyness, we need to learn from Paul the value of taking a break to recharge our spiritual batteries and reconnect with God.

We can learn a similar lesson from Jesus. He often went away from the crowds to pray. In fact, his ministry began after forty days of fasting and prayer in the desert. When his life on earth was nearly over, he spent time in prayer at Gethsemane.

Where can you find sabbath time in the midst of your busyness on this trip? How can you carve out that time without offending friends or hosts and without shirking any responsibilities? Write your ideas here.

BE STRONG AND COURAGEOUS

FOCUS: The journey's end

READ: Joshua 1:1-9

REFLECT

If you made a movie out of the Exodus journey, it would probably end with the Israelites finally entering the Promised Land after forty years in the desert. Can't you just imagine the credits rolling as the weary Israelites muster the energy to cross the Jordan River and enter the land of milk and honey?

Or maybe you imagine a fairy tale, the last words of which are, "And they all lived happily ever after."

Either way, the banks of the Jordan seem like the right place to end the story.

But the journey doesn't end there. It continues to this day. Good times and bad times lay ahead for the Israelites; both joy and suffering were just around the bend—and so was God. In fact, God told Joshua, "As I was with Moses, so I will be with you; I will not fail you or forsake you" (**Joshua 1:5b**).

But there was a catch: God expected the Israelites to follow his law, to meditate on it day and night. When they failed to do so (as they did throughout the Books of Judges, Samuel, Kings, and Chronicles), they fell into a cycle of oppression and distress followed by deliverance and redemption.

REACT

Today, we come to the end of our journey together, much like the Israelites ended their journey on the banks of the Jordan. We'll soon go our separate ways, just as the tribes of Israel settled in various parts of the Promised Land. When we do, we'll recognize—by its absence—the incredible strength that we have when we're together.

Fortunately, we can keep tapping into that strength by staying connected with one another after this trip ends. And even when our paths take us in different directions, we still have the promise from today's passage: "Be strong and courageous; do not be frightened or dismayed, for the LORD your God is with you wherever you go" (**Joshua 1:9**).

Prayer Focus

Pray for strength and courage on the road ahead.

Where will your path lead you when this trip ends? What specific actions can you take to tap into the strength that this group provides through the power of the Holy Spirit? Make some notes here.

Notes

JESUS STANDARD TIME

FOCUS: Dealing with schedule changes and other surprises

READ: Matthew 9:18-26

REFLECT

This story starts with an interruption. As Jesus was teaching about new wine and old wineskins, a synagogue leader came up to him with an urgent request: His daughter had died, and he begged Jesus to restore her to life.

Jesus immediately left for the man's house, but his interruption was interrupted—a bleeding woman appeared and asked for healing. He healed her and then took care of the leader's daughter. And then he was interrupted yet again! (See **Matthew 9:27.**) In fact, if you read all of **Matthew 9,** you'll see nothing but one interruption after another.

Yet Jesus never complained. He cared more about people and their problems than clocks and calendars. He was on a mission, but he wasn't on a schedule. He was on Jesus Standard Time.

REACT

Back home, we can easily become slaves to clocks and calendars. Our schedules are often so jam-packed that we don't have time to hit the snooze button, take an unexpected phone call, or even miss a traffic light on the way to school or work.

Schedules are important on mission trips, too, especially when we have to catch a plane or meet to travel to a worksite. But we're here to be servants to people, not slaves to schedules. We shouldn't focus so much on getting to the next activity that we miss the opportunities right here and now to be in service and fellowship.

Are you operating on Jesus Standard Time on this trip? What about the balance of priorities have you learned that you can take home with you? Write your thoughts on the next page.

Prayer Focus

Spend some (unmeasured) time in prayer for the place you are serving and the people who are around you right now. Push aside thoughts of yesterday and tomorrow, of things past and things to come.

Notes

BURNING BUSHES

FOCUS: Watching for chances to serve

READ: Exodus 3:1-10

REFLECT

The third chapter of Exodus tells the familiar story of Moses' encounter with God in a burning bush. Some people who read this story focus on how a bush can burn without charring. Others focus on the long list of excuses Moses comes up with to try to avoid doing what God is asking.

Those points are important, but another part of the story often gets overlooked: Moses' decision to approach the burning bush in the first place. He didn't have to step forward, and other people might have avoided doing so.

Elizabeth Barrett Browning described that decision her poem *Aurora Leigh*:

> Earth's crammed with heaven,
> And every common bush afire with God;
> And only he who sees takes off his shoes;
> The rest sit round it and pluck blackberries.

> **Prayer Focus**
>
> Pray that God will give you the eyes to see the miracles all around you.

REACT

When we put down your Bible and return to the modern world, we can easily wonder why miracles don't happen anymore like they did in the Bible. But maybe they do. Maybe we're just too busy plucking blackberries (or pressing buttons on a BlackBerry—or talking on a cell phone or listening to an iPod) to notice.

What about you? On this trip, have you discovered that every place is afire with God? Have you seen and taken off your shoes, or have you sat around and plucked blackberries? Make some notes below about the times on this trip when you've felt the presence of God. Return to this page on future days to make additional notes.

STILL, SMALL VOICE

FOCUS: Listening for God

READ: 1 Kings 19:1-18

REFLECT

In **1 Kings 18,** Elijah became a hero by defeating the prophets of Baal and convincing the Israelites to return to God. But his moment of triumph didn't last long. By the next chapter, he was literally running for his life and wishing he was dead (an interesting paradox, when you stop to think about it).

As he ran, an angel of the Lord took care of him, providing him food and water and guiding his steps. And so he traveled for forty days and forty nights until he reached Horeb, the mountain of God, where the Lord would pass by.

Elijah stood at the mouth of a cave, watching as a mighty wind, an earthquake, and a fire struck the mountain. But God was not in the wind or in the earthquake or in the fire. Instead, God was in the still, small voice that followed. That gentle voice calmed Elijah and enabled him to return to doing God's work.

REACT

Mission trips can be loud, chaotic, and even a little scary at times. After rough days (or even successful ones), we may long for the chance to hide in a cave like Elijah did.

Daily devotional times are a great opportunity to listen for the still, small voice of God amid the hubbub of a busy schedule.

How is your devotional life on this trip? Are you able to find the setting you need to center your thoughts on God? Make some notes about what you're hearing—or what you need to do in coming days to draw closer to God.

Prayer Focus

Pray that God's still, small voice might break through the noise that's all around you today.

Notes

AT THE LORD'S FEET

FOCUS: Letting the message you're sharing reach you

READ: Luke 10:38-42

REFLECT

What would you do if Jesus came to dinner at your home? When Jesus visited the home of Mary and Martha, the two sisters had different ideas about what to do.

Mary sat at the Lord's feet, soaking up his parables and life-changing lessons. Martha played the perfect hostess, working in the kitchen and leaving only to complain that Mary wasn't helping out. (If you have a brother or sister, you can probably sympathize!)

Jesus quickly set Martha straight. Mary had made the right decision, he said quietly, not Martha.

Luke's Gospel doesn't record Martha's reaction, but we encounter the sisters again in **John 11,** when Jesus raised their brother, Lazarus, from the dead. This time, Martha was not in the kitchen; she was out on the road, boldly proclaiming her faith in Jesus. "I believe that you are the Messiah, the Son of God, the one coming into the world," she said (**John 11:27**).

Martha had joined her sister at the Lord's feet.

REACT

Mission trips tend to turn people into Marthas. We spend our days serving other people and often spend our evenings doing the sorts of chores we avoid back home: cooking, washing dishes, sweeping floors, and so forth. Some of us even make up our own beds!

Those things are all good, of course; but sometimes we need to choose what is better. Sometimes we need to listen to what we're saying to those we serve—and listen for what God is saying to us on this trip.

On the next page, note the times during this trip when you have been able to hear God's voice most clearly. Also make note of what God has said to you.

Prayer Focus

Pray for "Mary moments" during the rest of this trip, moments when you can move beyond work and spend time at the Lord's feet.

Notes

TWENTY-FOUR FEET

FOCUS: Serving the ungrateful

READ: John 13:1-17

REFLECT

The night of the Last Supper, Jesus surprised the disciples by whipping off his cloak and kneeling down to wash their feet.

As usual, Peter hogged the spotlight—and missed the point. He protested that he wouldn't let Jesus wash his feet but then asked Jesus to wash his hands and his head as well.

Of course, the lesson that Jesus was teaching was not about physical cleanliness. By washing the disciples' feet, he was demonstrating servanthood.

We modern readers may understand that lesson (even if we fail to act on it), but we often miss a more subtle point in this story: Jesus washed the feet of *all* the disciples—including Judas. Even though he knew that Judas would betray him and even though Judas had done nothing to deserve such good treatment, Jesus stooped down and washed his feet anyway. He did the same for Peter, who would later deny Jesus three times (just as Jesus had predicted).

That's just the way Jesus was—and the way we should be.

REACT

If you wash enough feet, you'll get kicked in the face (not literally, let's hope). You'll encounter someone who's ungrateful, who resents your interference in his or her life, who throws away the gift you offer. When you get that response, you can give up on the person or you can love the person anyway. You can use the ingratitude as an excuse to give up on people or as a reason to serve people with even more love. No one can doubt which choice Jesus made.

Have you encountered ungrateful people on this trip? Write down what they did and how you reacted. How did your reaction make the situation better or worse? What could you do differently next time?

Serving people who are ungrateful or seem undeserving can be hard. Pray for the wisdom to see beyond people's negative attitudes and actions and for the strength to love them anyway.

Notes

THANKSGIVING IS OUR DIALECT

FOCUS: Gossip's potential to destroy the group

READ: Ephesians 5:1-21

REFLECT

Paul's letter to the church at Ephesus is full of advice about Christian living. This chapter in particular lists all sorts of things that Christians should and shouldn't do.

Did you notice how much of Paul's advice relates to talking? He says we should avoid "obscenity, foolish talk, or coarse joking," be wary of "empty words," and "speak to one another with psalms, hymns, and spiritual songs." That last part may seem a little over the top, but Paul makes important points about how what we say reflects who we are.

The Message, a contemporary paraphrase of the Bible, makes **Ephesians 5:4** even more relevant to modern readers: "Though some tongues just love the taste of gossip, those who follow Jesus have better uses for language than that. Don't talk dirty or silly. That kind of talk doesn't fit our style. Thanksgiving is our dialect."

REACT

If there's anything we do on mission trips more than work, it's talk. We talk about the work we're doing, we talk about life back home, sports, food, TV shows, and one another ... and that area is where we get into trouble.

A childhood rhyme says, "Sticks and stones may break my bones, but words can never hurt me." But words do hurt. They hurt the subject of the gossip, they hurt the group as a whole, and they hurt the gossiper. As **James 1:26** says, "If any think they are religious, and do not bridle their tongues but deceive their hearts, their religion is worthless."

Is thanksgiving your dialect, or do you have trouble keeping a tight rein on your tongue? On the next page, write down some ways you can avoid saying things you'll later regret.

Notes

IF IT IS FROM GOD

FOCUS: Drawing on God's power

READ: Acts 5:27-39

REFLECT

After Jesus ascended into heaven, the disciples (which means "students") became apostles (which means something like "those who go forth"). And go forth they did! Peter and the other apostles healed the sick, boldly preached the gospel, and brought many people to Christ. By **Acts 4:4,** thousands of people had become believers.

The apostles' Spirit-led success upset the high priests and some jealous Sadducees (**Acts 5:17**). Some of them wanted to put the apostles to death, but Gamaliel—a Pharisee and renowned leader of the Law—knew better. If the source of the Christians' power was human, he said, they would surely fail. If the source was God, no one would be able to stop them.

Gamaliel was more correct than he knew. Saul, one of Gamaliel's students (**Acts 22:3**), became Paul, the apostle to the Gentiles and the author of much of the New Testament.

REACT

In setting out on this mission trip, you've gone from being a disciple to being an apostle, from a student to one who goes forth (although you'll still have to go back to school). Like the apostles in Acts, you've been empowered by the Spirit to spread the gospel to the ends of the earth (**Acts 1:8**).

That ability doesn't mean that things will always go smoothly, however. While you won't be dragged in front of the religious authorities or threatened with stoning, you probably will face obstacles in the days to come. When those problems occur, remember what Gamaliel told his fellow rabbis. And remember how his student Saul went from being Christianity's meanest persecutor to its leading promoter.

What kind of opposition from other people (either here or back home) prevents you from sharing your faith? How can you learn to view certain foes as potential friends? Make some notes on the next page.

Notes

POOR PAUL

FOCUS: Putting adversity in perspective

READ: 2 Corinthians 11:16 -31

REFLECT

Paul's second letter to the Corinthians deals with a major threat to his ministry. The church at Corinth had been infiltrated by people who were accusing Paul of being a liar, a thief, and a false prophet; and he felt compelled to respond. So he devoted much of this letter, including this remarkable passage, to defending his ministry.

Now, some people might accuse Paul of ignoring **Proverbs 16:18** ("Pride goes before destruction, a haughty spirit before a fall") or **Proverbs 29:23** ("A man's pride brings him low, but a man of lowly spirit gains honor"). But the only way Paul could prove himself to the Corinthian Christians was by boasting at length of his suffering. Nothing else could show his commitment to Christ.

REACT

Mission trips are lots of things, but they're not luxury vacations. We don't eat in five-star restaurants, find mints on our pillows, or spend afternoons lounging beside the pool. At times, in fact, we find ourselves suffering—and grumbling about it to anyone who will listen.

At those times, we need to remember Paul's words from **2 Corinthians 12:9b-10**:

> I will boast all the more gladly of my weaknesses, so that the power of Christ may dwell in me. Therefore I am content with weaknesses, insults, hardships, persecutions, and calamities for the sake of Christ; for whenever I am weak, then I am strong.

Do you use difficulties as chances to invite Christ into your life? Or do you allow them to become barriers to Christ's grace and power? How could the challenges you've faced on this trip be opportunities to glorify God? Make some notes on the next page.

Prayer Focus

Pray that God might give you the vision to see beyond short-term suffering to the long-term benefits of difficulties and challenges—both in your life and in the lives of those you're serving on this trip.

Notes

BETTER THAN JESUS' WORKS?

FOCUS: Strengthened by faith in Jesus

READ: John 14:1-14

REFLECT

If you've read much of John's Gospel, you know that he often writes in a poetic style that's beautiful to listen to but sometimes hard to understand. A good example of that style is this passage, which shows Jesus explaining to the disciples—five times—that he and God are one. "Whoever has seen me has seen the Father," he said. "I am in the Father and the Father is in me" (**John 14:9, 11**).

In fact, you see Jesus making this point so many times that you can easily miss his next teaching, which is amazing: Anyone who believes in him will do the things that he has done. In fact, anyone who has faith, Jesus said, "will do greater works than these, because I am going to the Father" (**John 14:12**).

Even greater than Jesus' works? Yes! The Lord expects his followers to carry on the work he began during his earthly ministry and to take his work to the next level. Through the Holy Spirit, Christ empowers his followers to do so.

REACT

Mission trips like this one bring the world's problems into focus for us. And those problems—poverty, devastation, and all the rest—can seem overwhelming. Making a difference in a single life, much less an entire community, can seem as impossible as emptying the ocean with a teaspoon or moving a mountain one boulder at a time.

Of course, Jesus had something to say about mountains: "If you have faith the size of a mustard seed, you will say to this mountain, 'Move from here to there,' and it will move; and nothing will be impossible for you" (**Matthew 17:20b**).

As you go out to work today and in the coming days, remember that Christ doesn't just call us into service; he also empowers us. When we put our faith in him, we can do not only what he did but also even greater things.

How have you felt Jesus' power during this trip or other mission trips? Make some notes on the next page, and add to the list in the coming days.

Prayer Focus

Pray that your faith might be strengthened so that your effectiveness may be increased.

Notes

THE GREATEST

FOCUS: Maneuvering for positions of prestige

READ: Mark 10:35-45

REFLECT

Those silly disciples! After following Jesus all over creation and listening to him preach about servanthood, James and John came to him with a bold request: "Grant us to sit, one at your right hand and one at your left, in your glory" (**Mark 10:37**).

Jesus had to have been frustrated with the brothers. They had obviously missed one of the key points of his message: In his kingdom, greatness would come from being a servant—not from wealth, prestige, family connections, or special favors.

But Jesus wasn't the only one who became upset with James and John. Verse 41 says that the other disciples grew indignant. Mark doesn't say why, but we can assume that their anger stemmed from wanting best seats in Jesus' throne room too; they just hadn't been bold enough—or silly enough—to make a similar request.

REACT

We can easily criticize James and John. Knowing how the story ends, we understand that their request is completely out of line. We would never seek recognition that way.

Or would we?

Think back over the past few days. Have you ever grabbed for power or prestige by jumping to the head of a serving line, perhaps? by claiming the best seat on the way to a work site? Have you avoided doing hard or dirty jobs fit for only servants? Have you eagerly expected praise for the good things you have done? Have you forgotten that you're on this trip to serve, not to be served?

On the next page, take some notes about those times; recommit yourself to following Jesus' example during the rest of the trip.

Prayer Focus

Pray for forgiveness if you
need it and for the heart of
a servant, which we all need.

Notes

BUT THERE IS A GOD

FOCUS: Keeping the focus on Christ

READ: Daniel 2:25-30

REFLECT

King Nebuchadnezzar of Babylon had a disturbing dream. He asked his court astrologers to explain what it meant, but he wouldn't tell them what the dream was all about. (Clever, huh?)

Not surprisingly, they couldn't interpret the dream. So he threatened to kill them, as well as Daniel and his friends Hananiah, Mishael and Azariah, young Jews who were among the king's wise men (and who were better known as Shadrach, Meshach, and Abednego). Before the king went through with the executions, however, Daniel offered to take a crack at figuring out the dream's meaning.

Daniel gave a correct interpretation, of course, which takes up the rest of Chapter 2. But the important thing, at least for us, is not what Daniel said about the dream but what he said about God. No man can interpret your dream, he said, but there is a God who can. (In fact, God had revealed the mystery to Daniel the previous night as he and his friends prayed.) And Daniel gave all the glory to God.

REACT

When young people go out into the mission field, people tend to pour on the praise like pancake syrup. We all like to be recognized for our hard work, of course; and there's nothing wrong with accepting thanks for a job well done. But like Daniel, we need to remember the source of our power: God. The Lord can do far more for the people here than we could ever do, and God will still be here working long after we've returned home.

Have you found yourself failing to give God the glory on this trip? How might you gently redirect people's praise from yourself and our group toward God? Make some notes on the next page.

Prayer Focus

Pray that you might become transparent so that the people you serve can see Jesus in you.

Notes

MANNA AND QUAIL

FOCUS: Mission trip food

READ: Exodus 16:1-21

REFLECT

After crossing the Red Sea, the Israelites were free, safe from their Egyptian oppressors, and hungry—very hungry. They were so hungry, in fact, that they started dreaming about being back in Egypt with pots of meat and all the food they wanted. It was as if slavery had been some kind of all-you-can-eat buffet. (For a different perspective, read **Exodus 1:8-14.**)

In the midst of their complaining, God promised to send food and plenty of it. God would dole out the food one day at a time (with a double portion on the sixth day so that nobody will have to work on the sabbath). The catch was that the Israelites weren't allowed to save up food. They would get just what they needed to survive—nothing more, nothing less.

REACT

When we say the Lord's Prayer, we ask God to give us our "daily bread." But the reality is that most of us have access to a whole lot more food than one day's worthy of bread. Our pantries contain all sorts of food; and if we don't find anything there we like, we can always order a pizza or hit the nearest burger place.

Such is not the case on mission trips. Out here, we usually don't get to decide what to eat or when to eat it. Instead, we have to rely on other people to give us our daily bread—whether it's burgers and fries, rice and beans, or something that's not quite unidentifiable but tastes sort of like chicken. What a great lesson in trusting God to provide for us day by day!

Has your stomach been rumbling, and have you been grumbling? What does "eating to live instead of living to eat" mean? Do you have any other areas of your life where you need to rely on God to take care of your daily needs? Make some notes on the next page.

Prayer Focus

Pray that God might give you just what you need today—and just for today.

Notes

OH, THOSE POOR PEOPLE!

FOCUS: The difference between poor and pathetic

READ: Ecclesiastes 5:10-20; Philippians 4:11-13

REFLECT

If Ecclesiastes were written today, it would probably be called something like *Ten Easy Lessons on How NOT to Be Happy*. The early part of the Book summarizes the many ways the author, who calls himself the Teacher, tried to find happiness and failed. One of those ways, as this passage describes, was by getting rich.

Despite amassing silver and gold and "the treasure of kings and of provinces" (**Ecclesiastes 2:8**), the Teacher realized that he was no happier than a common laborer. His wealth kept him up at night, while the sleep of laborers was "sweet, whether they [ate] little or much" (**Ecclesiastes 5:12**).

But the real problem was not the Teacher's wealth. It was his inability (or unwillingness) to find satisfaction with his lot in life. Paul talks about that predicament in the Philippians passage. Through Christ, Paul says, we can learn to be content in any situation, full or hungry, rich or poor.

REACT

Mission trips often take us to parts of the world, or parts of our own country, where people have little money and few material possessions. As we look at their simple homes, worn-out clothing, and unpaved streets, our first reaction is often, "Oh, those poor people!"

We have to remember the difference between being poor and being pathetic. While we should never glamorize poverty, we also shouldn't assume that people are less happy or that their lives are less complete because they have little material wealth.

We should remember Jesus' words from the Sermon on the Mount: "Do not judge, so that you may not be judged" (**Matthew 7:1**). After all, those people you're feeling sorry for may be feeling sorry for you as you lug around a heavy suitcase or worry about getting your expensive sneakers dirty on their unpaved streets!

Do you find yourself making judgments or assumptions about the people here because of their lack of money and possessions? Do you do the same thing back home? Commit yourself instead to looking for gladness of heart, and record your commitment in the writing space.

Prayer Focus

Pray that you might find contentment in your own situation and that you might see the contentment of the people in this place.

Notes

MOPPING FOR JESUS

FOCUS: How chores advance the gospel

READ: Acts 6:1-7

REFLECT

Widows in New Testament times led pretty rough lives. There was no Social Security or Medicare. If widows had no sons to care for them, their only means of support was charity. So the early church committed itself to taking care of these vulnerable women. **1 Timothy 5:3-16,** in fact, gives detailed instructions on care for widows.

As the church grew, however, the Twelve (the original group Jesus called to lead the church) became so absorbed with spreading the gospel that they didn't pay enough attention to their ministry to widows. When a group of Greek-speaking converts complained, the Twelve decided that they would neglect neither ministry.

Instead, they appointed a group called the Seven to care for the widows while continuing to devote themselves to "prayer and to serving the word" (**Acts 6:4**). As a result, both the church and the widows prospered.

REACT

No job on a mission trip should be considered glamorous, but some jobs seem especially menial. It seems unlikely that chores such as floor mopping, bathroom cleaning, and dish washing could help spread the gospel. But they can.

Think about a worship service back home. The pastor and the choir or music team may get all the attention, but the services couldn't happen without the people who clean the sanctuary, print the bulletin, serve as ushers, fill Communion cups, and perform a bunch of other "menial" tasks.

It's the same way here. While the chores we do on trips such as this one may not seem important, they make seemingly more important work possible.

The passage from Acts emphasizes just how important behind-the-scenes work is. Rather than treat the Seven as inferiors, the Twelve prayed over them and laid hands on them, just like they were ministers of the gospel. The Seven were, in fact, equally ministers of the gospel.

Have you found it easy to do menial tasks on this trip, or have you found it difficult? Does knowing that chores do advance the gospel help you? Write your impressions here.

Prayer Focus

Pray that you might develop a true servant's heart, remembering these words of Jesus: "Whoever wants to be first must be last of all and servant of all" (**Matthew 9:35b**).

Notes

NAMES IN THE BOOK OF LIFE

FOCUS: Squabble mediation

READ: Philippians 4:2-9

REFLECT

Euodia and Syntyche appear in one verse in the Bible: **Philippians 4:2.** And it's not the sort of thing they'd want to brag about.

All the way from Rome, Paul had heard that the two Philippian women have been fighting—about what, we don't know. When he wrote an open letter to their church, he included a brief plea for them to patch things up. How's that for immortality?

Paul didn't stop there. He also plead with his companion (whom some translations name Syzygus, which is Greek for "companion"), another member of the church, to intercede in the fight.

Finally, Paul shared some advice about how to avoid conflict: Let your gentleness be evident to all. Don't be anxious. Focus on what is noble, right, and pure.

If only Euodia and Syntyche had followed this advice, they might be known for something other than being scolded by Paul.

REACT

When we start out on mission trips, we usually strive to be gentle and to focus on what is noble, right, and pure. But as the days wear on, getting cranky and picking fights with one another becomes easier.

So where are you right now? Are you like Euodia and Syntyche, embroiled in a fight that's attracted attention from beyond the group? Or are you like Paul's companion, able to mediate conflict between friends but just waiting for permission? If you're not where you'd like to be, what could you do to change? Make some notes on the next page.

Now, imagine that Paul is writing a letter to our group. What words of concern or encouragement might he include about you? Write your thoughts on the next page.

Notes

NO PLACE TO LAY HIS HEAD

FOCUS: Mission trip housing

READ: Matthew 8:18-23; Luke 2:1-7

REFLECT

Jesus never glossed over the challenges of being a disciple. If you want to follow me, he told potential followers, you need to sell all your possessions, give all your money to the poor, and even turn your back on your family. Nothing—not looks, not status, not education—counts more than total submission.

Nobody knows whether the scribe in **Matthew 8** had good looks, but he definitely had status and education. He was also brave enough to approach Jesus in a crowd and ask to be a disciple.

But was he brave enough to follow Jesus? Did he get in that boat with the other disciples in verse 23? We can't know for sure, because the Bible doesn't tell us.

What the Bible does tell us is that primitive conditions were no big deal for Jesus. His mention of having no place to lay his head reminds us of a time in his life when there was no room in the inn.

REACT

So, how did you sleep last night? Did you dream about being back home in your nice, soft bed?

Sleeping accommodations on trips like this one are usually pretty basic. Fluffy pillows or cushy mattresses aren't available. Nobody turns down the covers each morning or leaves a mint on your pillow. And you're probably sleeping a whole lot closer to a whole lot more people than you're accustomed to. Sometimes it may seem that there's no room to lay your head.

That difficulty is part of being a disciple. We're here to serve, not to sleep (although we do need to get enough sleep to make our service possible). And we can't serve many people lying on a cot or in a sleeping bag.

On the next page, make some notes about the sleeping arrangements on this trip. If you've had a tough time adjusting, brainstorm some ways you could make things better (short of relocating to the nearest four-star hotel).

OF FOOD AND FREEDOM

FOCUS: Keeping our freedoms in check

READ: Romans 14:13-21

REFLECT

The early Christians came to the church from two directions. Some were Jews, people who'd grown up striving to obey the commandments laid down in the Jewish Scriptures, including the dietary laws found in **Leviticus 11.** Others were Gentiles, people who found such rules strange and complicated.

Not surprisingly, tension existed between the two groups of believers. In fact, the leaders of the church had to call a special council, described in **Acts 15:1-35,** to decide which rules, if any, the Gentile Christians needed to follow. In the end, they decided that the Gentiles should be free of most Jewish dietary restrictions.

While Paul supported that decision, he also recognized that freedom comes with responsibility. As Paul argued in **Romans 14:14-15,** people who ate unclean food around Jewish Christians weren't acting out of love. Instead, they were destroying the work of God for the sake of food.

REACT

The people we're serving this week won't be offended by what we eat, but they could well be offended by what we wear. Certain cultures may consider fashions such as short shorts, spaghetti straps, and T-shirts with suggestive messages to be stumbling blocks.

So is our language. Words that seem OK in the halls at school may not be acceptable here. And it's not just what we say but how we say it. Some cultures may be offended by the loud, sarcastic, or abrasive tone of voice that many of us use when joking around with friends.

What's the solution? We should heed the words of Paul and "pursue what makes for peace and for mutual upbuilding" (**Romans 14:19**). By keeping our freedoms in check during this trip, we build up the kingdom of God rather than building up barriers between us and the people we're here to serve.

What freedoms do you need to keep in check? Do you need to offer counsel to a friend about his or her dress or language? Make some notes here, and make a commitment to act.

Prayer Focus

Pray that you become a building block, not a stumbling block, in the way you dress, talk, and act throughout the days ahead.

Notes

OVERFLOWING GRACE

FOCUS: Making an example of yourself

READ: 1 Timothy 1:12-17

REFLECT

Paul didn't pull any punches. In his open letters to various churches, he often criticized people, sometimes by name, for behavior that was contrary to the message of the gospel. Whether the issue was sexual immorality, false teachers, or divisions in the church, Paul spoke his mind clearly and forcefully. His letters have lots of exclamation points.

Paul could recognize sin because he himself was a sinner. In fact, according to this passage, he was "the worst of sinners," "a blasphemer, a persecutor, and a man of violence."

Yet God poured out grace on Paul. And so Paul spent the rest of his days praising the Lord with his words and with actions, sharing the good news that had transformed his life.

REACT

"The saying is sure and worthy of full acceptance, that Christ Jesus came into the world to save sinners."

Do those words from **1 Timothy 1:15** sound familiar? They're often used in affirmations of faith during worship services, although the rest of the sentence—"of whom I am the foremost"—usually gets left off. That critical omission changes the focus from "us sinners" to "those sinners."

But Paul recognized that we have to focus on ourselves before we can worry about others. We have to acknowledge what God has done for us before we can talk about what God can do for other people. In a mission setting, that attitude means being willing to open up to the people we're serving.

Rather than pretending to be a perfect Christian, a claim that no one can make, you should be honest about your doubts and your shortcomings. Only when people see the real you will they be able to see the real God.

On the next page, make some notes here about how God has helped you deal with the sin in your life. How can you tell your story during this trip?

Notes

Post-Trip Devotions

I MAY COME TO YOU WITH JOY

FOCUS: Planning your next journey

READ: Romans 15:23-33

REFLECT

When Paul wrote this message to the Roman church, he was probably on his third missionary journey. He was in or near Corinth, where he'd planted a strong Christian church in what was a pretty rough town. His work complete, he was looking ahead to the future—not to returning home but to continuing his mission work.

Although he'd already traveled thousands of miles during the past decade or so, Paul was looking forward to his next journey—his next two journeys, in fact. The first would be to Jerusalem, where he would deliver an offering to that city's Christians. The next would be to Rome and then, perhaps, to Spain. (Nobody's sure whether he got to Spain, but he did make it to Rome.)

REACT

While our missionary journey together is over, God's call to us continues. Leaving our mission gear on the shelf might be easy, but we should follow Paul's example and start planning now for the next journey. Whether our destination is close to home or on the other side of the globe, we find joy and refreshment whenever we serve God's people in the world.

What parts of this trip would you like to repeat?
Whom do you want to serve in the future?
Where? How? What's the first step you need to
take? Write your ideas here.

Prayer Focus

Pray that God might point
you toward your next
mission opportunity.

Notes

IT IS THE LORD!

FOCUS: Finding Jesus in everyday life

READ: John 21:1-14

REFLECT

After the Resurrection, Jesus didn't immediately ascend into heaven. Instead, according to **Acts 1:3,** he remained on earth for forty days. The Gospels record some of his post-Resurrection appearances, among them his appearance on the lakeshore in **John 21.**

The way John tells the story, seven disciples led by Peter had gone fishing. Despite trying all night, they hadn't caught a thing. Then, just as morning broke, a man shouted to them from the shore that they needed to throw their nets in on the other side of the boat. They followed his advice and immediately caught more fish than they could haul in. Only then did they realize that the man on the shore was Jesus.

The disciples' return to their boats after the Resurrection is no surprise. They had to eat, after all, and fishing was their livelihood. What is surprising is that they didn't recognize Jesus. This post-Resurrection appearance was not his first; John describes two previous appearances in Chapter 20.

Maybe the men were tired from fishing all night. Or maybe they all needed glasses. Or maybe, just maybe, they didn't expect Jesus to show up in such an ordinary place.

REACT

On mission trips, we can easily experience the presence of Christ. He's there in our prayers and our songs, our devotional time and our work projects.

When we return home, we may feel like we've left Christ back on the mission field. Rather than being a constant presence in our lives, he again becomes just our Sunday-morning Savior.

But Christ isn't the one who's changed. **Hebrews 13:8** says, "Jesus Christ is the same yesterday and today and forever." Instead, we're the ones who've changed—or maybe just changed back. Amid the ordinary concerns of school, work, sports, and chores, we forget to look for Christ. And so we don't find him.

Take a few minutes to jot down ways you experienced the presence of Jesus Christ on the mission trip. What could you do in your daily life to make him more than just a Sunday-morning Savior?

Prayer Focus

Pray that Jesus might continue to make his presence known in your daily life, even when you're doing homework, cleaning your room, flipping burgers, or fishing for your supper.

Notes

GREETINGS!

FOCUS: Keeping in touch with those we've served

READ: Romans 16:1-16

REFLECT

Paul's open letters to various churches are full of beautiful language (as in **1 Corinthians 13**) and complex theological arguments (like most of Romans). But mixed in with those timeless words are dozens of personal greetings.

In this passage, Paul sends greetings to twenty-four individuals in Rome, along with others he doesn't identify by name. Later in the chapter, he sends these Romans additional greetings from other Christians who are with him as he writes.

If you have a study Bible, it probably includes maps of Paul's missionary journeys, which look like big loops around the Mediterranean Sea. Paul's letters (and the personal greetings they contain) intersect those loops and pull them together, creating a web that connects Christians in communities from Jerusalem to Ephesus, Athens to Rome, people who were "tested and approved in Christ" (**Romans 16:10,** NIV).

REACT

Christians today are often guilty of drive-by mission work. We descend on a community, spend time working and starting relationships, and then return home, leaving those relationships behind. Even though it's easier than ever to communicate with people in distant places, we often struggle to maintain communication with those we've served.

Have you been in touch with people you met during our mission trip? If not, commit to writing a letter or e-mail today. You could address it to the entire community, as Paul did, or to a specific individual you connected with. Use the space on the next page to record ideas for greetings you'd like to send.

Prayer Focus

Pray for the ability to stay in touch with those you've served, spinning a web of connection just as Paul did nearly two thousand years ago.

Notes

REFLECTED GLORY

FOCUS: Bringing God home from the mission field

READ: Exodus 34:27-35; 2 Corinthians 3:12-18

REFLECT

The Exodus passage describes Moses' trip to Mount Sinai to receive the Ten Commandments for the second time. (He'd broken the first set of stone tablets in anger because the Israelites had started worshiping a golden calf.)

Moses didn't just go up the mountain and back in a single day; he spent forty days and nights in God's presence. When he came down from the mountain, his face was radiant, reflecting the glory of God. In fact, the Israelites were afraid to come near him; so he wore a veil to hide his glowing face.

In the passage from 2 Corinthians, Paul referred back to the Moses incident. But Paul argued that people who have been in God's presence shouldn't hide their faces. Instead, they should let their unveiled faces reflect the Lord's glory.

REACT

Our mission trip was something like Moses' visit to Mount Sinai—an extended time in the presence of God. When we returned home, God's reflected glory showed on our faces (along with signs that we didn't get enough sleep on the trip).

We've been to the mountaintop, a place many of our friends and family may never go, and we have a responsibility to tell others about our experience. While we shouldn't scare anybody by being too pushy or preachy, we shouldn't hide our faces either.

We should also remember something else: Moses' face lost some of its radiance when he left God's presence. He had to return to God again and again to recharge his spiritual batteries. We should do the same.

Have you shared God's reflected glory since you've arrived home? If not, commit now to doing so. What steps do you need to take in the coming weeks and months to recharge your spiritual batteries? Make some notes on the next page.

Prayer Focus

Pray that your family and friends might see God's glory reflected in you and that they too might choose to go to the mountaintop in the future.

Notes

ANGELS UNAWARES

FOCUS: Offering hospitality

READ: Deuteronomy 10:17-19; Hebrews 13:2

REFLECT

Some of the laws found in Old Testament books such as Leviticus and Deuteronomy seem strange to us modern readers. They probably seemed strange to the Israelites who had to follow them, too. For that reason, many of the laws came complete with explanations.

Take a look at **Leviticus 19:10,** for example: "Do not go over your vineyard a second time or pick up the grapes that have fallen. Leave them for the poor and the alien." That second sentence gives the reason for the rule.

It's the same with the passage from Deuteronomy about taking care of aliens. The Israelites were called to love outsiders not just because it was the right thing to do but also because they had been outsiders in Egypt.

Still, the Israelites had another reason to follow the rule. That tantalizing verse from Hebrews indicates that some people who thought they were entertaining strangers were actually entertaining angels in disguise!

REACT

During our mission trip, we relied on the hospitality of strangers, people who fed and housed and generally took care of us. Now that we're home, we should return the favor by paying it forward.

Like the ancient Israelites, we know the feeling of being strangers in a strange land; so we should heed those words from Deuteronomy. We should jump at the chance to feed or shelter people who come to our community on mission trips.

Has your family hosted visitors to our community? What was the experience like? What do you have to offer that would be helpful to a stranger? Make some notes on the next page.

Notes

Ready to Go

Pre-Service Devotions

THE LEAST OF MY FAMILY

FOCUS: God's strength strengthens us

READ: Judges 6:11-24; Psalm 28:7-8

REFLECT

If you were picking someone to be a hero, you probably wouldn't pick Gideon. As the Israelites cried out for someone to save them from the Midianites, Gideon hid in a shed, threshing wheat and wondering why God had abandoned his people.

When an angel appeared and called him a "mighty warrior" (a nice bit of irony), Gideon wasn't impressed. He knew he didn't have what it takes to be a hero. After all, he was the lowliest member of the weakest clan in the tribe of Manasseh.

But then Gideon heard God's own voice. "Go in the strength you have," God said. "Am I not sending you?" (**Judges 6:14,** NIV).

Those words eventually sunk in. Gideon became the mighty warrior that the angel had imagined. In fact, he went on to defeat the Midianites with just 300 men—and one great God—on his side.

REACT

When we look at the world's problems (or even at the problems of the community we'll serve), we can easily become overwhelmed. Who are we to think that we can address those problems? We certainly don't have the power, the money, or the wisdom to make much of a difference.

But we have something else: the strength of God. When the Lord sends us out to serve God's people, God empowers us just as God empowered Gideon.

Take some time to think about your own strengths and weaknesses. In what ways can you use your strengths to help the group? How do you need God to shore up your weak areas? Make some notes below.

Notes

HEARING THE CALL

FOCUS: God's call to the young

READ: 1 Samuel 3:1–4:1; 16:6-13

REFLECT

The sons of Eli the priest were evil men, stealing food intended for offerings and sleeping with women who served at the Tabernacle. Eli knew of their sins but did little to stop them. So God decided to raise up a new priest, someone who would honor, not disdain, God. That person was Samuel.

In this passage, God let Samuel in on the news. It took Samuel a while to realize that God was speaking to him; but when he finally understood, his reaction was confident: "Speak, for your servant is listening" (**1 Samuel 3:10**).

Eventually, Samuel would anoint David as king over Israel. Although both Samuel and David had obvious flaws, both were men after God's own heart, men who became heroes of the faith.

REACT

Samuel was still a boy in Chapter 3. Nobody knows how old he was, but a safe bet is around twelve years old. David was also young. He was the youngest boy in his family, so young that his father didn't even bring him in from tending sheep when Samuel came to visit.

But God wasn't concerned about their age, nor was God concerned about their appearance or height or other external characteristics. As God told Samuel, "mortals . . . look on the outward appearance, but the Lord looks at the heart" (**1 Samuel 16:7**).

Do you feel inadequate to serve God because of your age? What comfort can you take from the stories of Samuel and David? Make some notes on the next page.

Prayer Focus

Pray that when God looks at your heart, God might see the heart of a servant.

Notes

PUTTING FEET TO OUR FAITH

FOCUS: Showing faith through our actions

READ: James 2:14-19

REFLECT

In this passage, James deals with the age-old question of whether we're made right with God (justified) through our faith or through our actions. James's answer? Yes!

We have to have faith in God; but if we have true faith, it will show up in how we act. In fact, if our faith doesn't bear fruit, it is dead. Or, as Eugene Peterson paraphrases verse 17 in *The Message,* "Isn't it obvious that God-talk without God-acts is outrageous nonsense?"

It's sort of like being in love. Someone who's in love will want to spend time with the person he or she is in love with and give this person gifts. Those actions are natural outgrowths of love. Similarly, James says, acts of mercy (such as feeding the hungry and clothing the naked) are natural outgrowths of faith. And they, not faith alone, make us right with God.

REACT

Earlier in his Book, James urges his readers not just to listen to the Word of God but also to do what it says (**James 1:22**). We'll be following God during our work project. We'll take all we've learned in worship, Sunday school, and youth activities and distill it down into acts of service to other people. In doing so, we'll make ourselves right with God while making our world a little better.

Think about the work projects you'll be doing. How are those projects outgrowths of your faith? How can they help you share your beliefs with the people you serve? Make some notes on the next page.

Prayer Focus

Pray that our work project might give you the chance to share, and strengthen, your faith.

Notes

JESUS IN DISGUISE

FOCUS: Serving Christ by serving people

READ: Matthew 25:31-46

REFLECT

A lot of us can't let go of our third-grade Sunday school Jesus: that gentle, smiling friend to children, sheep, and other small animals. But that image shows only one side of Jesus.

This passage from Matthew's Gospel shows another side. Here, Jesus sits on his throne in glory and judges all the people on earth, dividing them into two groups: sheep and goats. The sheep—those who have fed the hungry, welcomed the stranger, clothed the naked, cared for the sick, and visited the prisoner—receive places in his heavenly kingdom. The goats—those who have ignored the needs of others—receive everlasting punishment in "the eternal fire prepared for the devil and his angels" (**Matthew 25:41**).

It's enough to make us want to go back to third grade—or to start serving God's children.

REACT

Beyond visions of heavenly rewards and eternal punishment, the parable of the sheep and the goats makes a point that relates to our coming project: When we serve people, we serve Christ. The reverse, of course, is also true.

Mother Theresa, who ministered for many years to the poor and dying in Calcutta, India, often said that the people she served were "Jesus in disguise." That belief made her ministry one of love, not just service.

During our work project, how will seeing Christ in the people we serve make a difference in our attitudes and approach to service? Make some notes on the next page.

Prayer Focus

Pray for the ability to focus on Jesus, not just his disguises, during our work project.

Notes

WALL BUILDERS

FOCUS: God equips those whom God calls

READ: Nehemiah 3:1-12

REFLECT

In 588 B.C., King Nebuchadnezzar of Babylon conquered Judah and its capital city, Jerusalem. He destroyed Jerusalem's walls and took its leading citizens away into exile. (You can read all the gory details in **2 Kings 25:1-21.**)

About 150 years later, Nehemiah, a son of the Exile, traveled to Jerusalem to rebuild the city's walls. These walls, he knew, were essential to both the city's defense and its sense of well-being. As he said in **Nehemiah 2:17,** "Come, let us rebuild the wall of Jerusalem, so that we may no longer suffer disgrace."

Nehemiah 3, part of which you've just read, lists the leaders of the teams that rebuilt Jerusalem's walls (in 52 days). The list doesn't make for very exciting reading until you notice something remarkable: None of the people listed were professional wall builders. Instead, they were priests, rulers, goldsmiths, perfume makers, and servants. God can truly use anyone to achieve God's purposes.

REACT

If you think about our group and about yourself, you might easily decide that we aren't capable of accomplishing what we plan to do on our work project. After all, we're just a bunch of teenagers and amateurs, not professional missionaries. Yet we can accomplish great things with God's help, just as Nehemiah and his army of wall-builders did.

An old saying among church leaders is, "God doesn't call the equipped; God equips the called." We have been called to serve God's people on our work project, and God can equip us to serve effectively.

What skills do you need God to equip you with for our service project? How might God use you to equip other team members? Make some notes on the next page.

Prayer Focus

Pray that God's gracious hand might be on our group as we go out to serve God's people. (See **Nehemiah 2:18.**)

Notes

Ready to Go

Post-Service Devotions

PLANTING SEEDS

FOCUS: Doing our part and letting God do God's part

READ: 1 Corinthians 3:1-11

REFLECT

Many people think Christianity started breaking into denominations with the Great Schism of 1054 (when the breach between Eastern Orthodox churches and the Roman Catholic Church happened). But cracks were already visible when Paul wrote this letter to the church at Corinth around A.D. 55.

Paul had heard reports that the Corinthians were arguing among themselves about whom they should follow. Some said Paul, some said Apollos, some said Cephas (Peter), and some said—always a good answer—Jesus.

In Chapter 1 and again in this passage, Paul tried to show how foolish the Corinthians were acting. After all, he and Apollos were just servants in charge of little pieces of a monumental "gardening" job. Yes, Paul had planted the seed of faith in the Corinthians and Apollos did water it, but it was God who made it grow.

REACT

When we undertake work projects, we sometimes don't see those projects through from start to finish. We build on the work that previous groups have done, or we begin work for other people to complete.

We're like workers on an assembly line, adding a few parts to what will eventually be a comfortable house or a beautiful garden or a new Christian. Even though we may never see the final product roll off the assembly line, we can rest assured that we've played an important role in the work.

But we should always remember that God plays the most important part: powering the assembly line and enabling us to serve God's people in the world.

Prayer Focus

Pray for those who will build on the work we did during our project and for those who laid the foundation for our efforts.

How do you feel, knowing that we were part of a project much bigger than ourselves? Did you have difficulty leaving the work unfinished? Do you feel better realizing that others will follow us? Make some notes below.

Notes

THEY NAMED HIM OBED

FOCUS: Long-term impacts of short-term service

READ: Ruth 4:13-22

REFLECT

The Book of Ruth seems out of place in the Old Testament. It contains no prophecy and little theology, no stories about kings or commandments or the coming messiah.

Instead, Ruth is a love story. The short book of only four chapters tells the story of Ruth, a Moabite woman who remained devoted to her late husband's mother, followed her to Bethlehem, and fell in love with a wealthy farmer named Boaz.

So why is this book in the Bible? We don't find out until the last word of the last verse of the last chapter. There we discover that Ruth would be the great-grandmother of King David and thus an ancestor of Jesus Christ. (See **Matthew 1:5-6.**) Her seemingly insignificant life is far more significant than she or any of her contemporaries could have imagined.

REACT

We live in a society that expects quick results. We eat instant oatmeal, fast-food burgers, and microwave popcorn. We surf the Net on broadband connections and watch video-on-demand. We participate in church work projects and quickly see...well, maybe not.

We don't always see quick results from service projects like the one we just completed. Oh sure, we see the immediate results of our efforts; but we don't see—and will probably never see—the ultimate impact.

The work you have done and the example you have set may have changed the life of a person like Ruth. And that seemingly insignificant person may someday become far more significant than anyone (except God) can imagine.

Did you make a particular connection with anyone during our work project (including another member of our group)? How might you continue to encourage that person in the weeks and months to come? Write your thoughts on the next page.

Pray for the friends, family members, Sunday school teachers, and other people who have helped shape your faith walk. Then pray that God might use your service to shape the faith walk of another person, perhaps a seemingly insignificant person like Ruth.

Notes

GOOD SEED AND BAD SEED

FOCUS: Success comes only in time

READ: Matthew 13:24-30; Ecclesiastes 3:1-8

REFLECT

When we read Jesus' parables about the kingdom of heaven, we sometimes get lost in the references to wheat, mustard seeds, and vineyards. Of course, Jesus used agricultural images because his audience could relate to them. Since most of us aren't farmers, we have to do a little extra translating to understand Jesus' meaning.

In the story from Matthew's Gospel, a farmer—whom we'll call God—has planted some wheat seed in a field. Soon, his enemy—whom we'll call Satan—comes along and sows weeds among the wheat. (Scholars say these weeds were probably a plant called darnel, which looks a lot like wheat when it's young but not when it matures.)

The farmer's servants want to pull up the weeds right away, but the wise farmer knows it's better to wait. There is a time to plant and a time to uproot, and harvest time has yet to come.

REACT

We aren't farmers, but we planted seeds during our work project. Some will grow and bear fruit. Others may not.

It's tempting to want to return to our worksite and see which seeds are prospering; but we need to remember that growth happens on God's schedule, not on ours. At this stage, only God can separate the wheat from the weeds. Only at harvest time can we mortals tell the difference. The best we can do now is to be patient and, while we're waiting, continue to plant seeds.

Now that you're home, how can you continue the seed-planting you did during our work project? What can you do to nurture the seeds you've already planted? Make some notes on the next page.

Notes

FOR THIS REASON I KNEEL

FOCUS: Staying connected in prayer

READ: Ephesians 3:14-21

REFLECT

Paul invested a lot of himself in Ephesus. He visited the city briefly during his first missionary journey, leaving behind his friends Priscilla and Aquila (**Acts 18:19-21**) to develop the church there. He returned again on his third missionary journey, this time staying for more than two years.

During those years, according to **Acts 19,** Paul preached so much in both the synagogue and a local lecture hall that everyone in the region heard the Word of God. Eventually, however, he got chased out of town by the followers of the Greek god Artemis.

But Paul wasn't through with the Ephesian Christians. He stayed in touch with them over the years, and eventually Paul or one of his disciples wrote them the letter that became the Book of Ephesians. The passage you've read describes the hopes he had for them, as well as the faith he had that God would fulfill those wishes.

REACT

What's interesting about Paul's relationship with the Ephesians is that he kept in touch with them through letters and through prayer. He maintained a three-way relationship among himself, the Ephesians, and God, a relationship whose sole purpose was to strengthen the Ephesians' faith. He wanted them to understand "how wide and long and high and deep is the love of Christ" (**Ephesians 3:18,** NIV).

We can maintain similar relationships with the people we met during our work project. Consider committing yourself to writing or e-mailing some of the people you met and to praying for them regularly. By doing so, you'll remind them (and yourself) just how wide and long and high and deep Christ's love truly is.

On the next page, write down some ways you can stay in touch with the people you met. List specific needs you can pray for. Think about composing a prayer based on **Ephesians 3.**

Prayer Focus

Pray for those you
encountered during our
work project, for the needs
you saw, and for the needs
that were kept hidden.

Notes

WHAT DOES THE LORD REQUIRE?

FOCUS: Setting priorities

READ: Amos 5:21-24; Micah 6:6-8

REFLECT

In modern times, we tend to think that prophecy means predicting the future. But prophets talk as much about today as tomorrow. They're just as concerned about God's will for the present as they are about God's plans for the future.

We can see that concern in the famous passages you've just read. According to Micah and Amos, God was tired of burnt offerings, religious assemblies, and even songs of praise. What the Lord desired most of all was for God's people to roll up their sleeves, get out into the world, and make a difference.

REACT

When we're at home, we're often bombarded by competing priorities. Homework, jobs, chores, church, sports, and school activities demand pieces of our time. And when we do get a break, we have to choose between a dozen movies at the multiplex, 100 channels on the television, and millions of sites on the Internet.

Work projects are so much easier. Our tasks are defined, and all of those priorities back home tend to fade into the background. For a brief moment in time, we know just what the Lord, along with our group leaders, requires of us.

How can you bring some of that simplicity and certainty back home? And, more importantly, how can you do what the Lord requires of you every day, not just during big work projects? Make some notes here.

Topical Index